I0018008

Google Drive Tutorial Guide

The Definitive User Manual To Master
Drive with Illustrations

By

Isaac Alejo

Copyright ©2023 Isaac Alejo,

All rights reserved

Table of Content

INTRODUCTION

In an increasingly interconnected realm, a particular digital storage solution emerges as a groundbreaking answer for efficiently managing your various documents and information. With its inventive data storage, arrangement, and sharing strategy, this solution has significantly altered how we conduct our tasks, gain knowledge, and interact.

Just picture having all your crucial files safely retained within a centralized hub, from textual documents and data tables to visually engaging slideshows and multimedia content. The era of being concerned about misplaced physical storage devices or restricted local storage capacity has become a thing of the past. Thanks to the cloud-based storage offered by this solution, your information remains within reach at any given moment, irrespective of your physical location, provided you are connected to the internet.

Whether you find yourself navigating academic assignments, participating in collaborative professional projects, or striving for a more streamlined approach to handling personal records, the content of this resource caters to your specific requirements. Within these pages you will uncover the methods for real-time collaboration with peers, colleagues, or acquaintances while preserving version history and safeguarding the integrity of your work. This solution transcends mere storage; it presents itself as a dynamic platform that fosters teamwork and elevates productivity. So, whether you are a tech-proficient expert aiming to refine your workflow, a scholar searching for a contemporary educational strategy, or an individual endeavoring to simplify your digital existence, this guide serves as your comprehensive manual for fully tapping into the potential of this solution. Brace yourself to utilize the capabilities of cloud-oriented storage, efficient organization, and collaborative expertise as we embark on an expedition through the pragmatic facets of this indispensable instrument.

CHAPTER 1: WHAT IS GOOGLE DRIVE?

Google is not merely a cloud storage solution that relieves your computer from the burden of holding large amounts of gigabytes. It serves as a hub that connects various Google Suite applications, providing a space to utilize essential apps like Docs, Sheets, and Slides while also serving as a storage space for your files.

What is Google Drive?

Google Drive is a versatile cloud-based storage and collaboration platform developed by Google. It is a virtual repository for various digital files, including documents, images, videos, and more. This innovative service allows users to store their files securely online and access them from anywhere with an internet connection. But Google Drive's capabilities extend beyond mere storage; it offers a suite of collaborative tools that transform how individuals and teams work together on projects and share information.

At its core, Google Drive provides users with a generous amount of free storage space, allowing them to upload files and documents of different formats. The synchronized nature of the service ensures that modifications made to a file on one device are instantly reflected across all devices connected to the same Google account. This seamless synchronization eliminates manual transfers and fosters a smooth workflow, regardless of whether you're using a computer, smartphone, or tablet.

One of the standout features of Google Drive is its suite of office applications, including Google Docs (word processing), Google Sheets (spreadsheets), and Google Slides (presentation software). These applications enable users to create and edit content directly within the browser and allow real-time collaboration. Multiple individuals can work on the same document simultaneously, seeing changes made by others in real-time and even engaging in discussions through integrated comment threads. This real-time collaboration fosters a dynamic and efficient work environment, particularly for remote teams or those across different locations.

Security and privacy are paramount concerns regarding digital storage, and Google Drive addresses these with various security measures. These include data encryption for transit and at rest, two-factor authentication for account access, and advanced sharing controls. Users can choose who can access their files and whether they can view, edit, or comment on them.

Features of Google Drive

- **Synchronize Your Files Seamlessly:** Google Drive offers a convenient method to synchronize files across various devices, including desktop computers, laptops, smartphones, and tablets. Manual file transfers become unnecessary, as your data is synchronized with the cloud storage. You can seamlessly synchronize a range of content, such as photos, videos, documents, and more, using Google Drive. Furthermore, it simplifies file sharing with family, friends, and colleagues.
  Download the Google Drive app, log in with your Google account, and select which items you wish to synchronize.

  Once your files are synced with Google Drive, you can access them from any device at anytime. The need for manual transfers is eliminated, as files are automatically harmonized with the cloud storage.

- **Efficiently Store in Google Drive:** The "Save to Google Drive Chrome Extension" presents a swift and uncomplicated means of saving web content directly to your Google Drive. It saves time and eliminates the need to download files to your computer before uploading them to Google Drive.
  The extension's usage is intuitive and straightforward. A simple right-click on the desired content followed by selecting "Save to Google Drive" will promptly upload the content to your Google Drive.

  This powerful and user-friendly tool lets you store documents, images, audio, and videos directly into your Google Drive without departing from your browser.

  Additionally, the extension can be customized to save content into designated folders on your Drive, including shared folders, streamlining your content organization.

- **Transform PDFs into Docs:** PDF files are widely used, ensuring consistent appearance across different devices. However, PDFs pose challenges for easy editing, hindering updates or modifications. Thankfully, Google Drive facilitates PDF editing by converting them into Docs. Right-clicking a PDF file in Google Drive prompts the option to open it with Google Docs. This process is quick, taking just a few seconds. Once opened, the file becomes editable in Google Docs, enabling effortless edits and collaborative work. Nevertheless, intricate fonts and formatting in complex PDFs may translate poorly in Google Docs.

Online PDF editors like PDF filler can be employed for seamless PDF editing without complications. This tool simplifies modifications, allowing text addition, deletion, signature fields, and more.

- **Save Gmail Attachments:** This functionality proves particularly handy for individuals who frequently receive numerous emails containing images or attachments. Rather than individually downloading each attachment, you can swiftly and effortlessly store all of them in Drive with a single action. It simplifies the organization and monitoring of attachments, ensuring crucial files are always noticed.

  To utilize this feature, click on the "Drive icon" adjacent to the attachment or image, opt for "Add to Drive," and you're done. Your attachment or image will be automatically preserved and systematically arranged within your Drive, accessible anytime.

- **Work Offline:** A notable advantage of Google Drive is its enabling offline work. It means you need not fret about data loss if your internet connection falters. It proves especially advantageous when you're moving and lack access to a dependable internet connection.

  To engage in offline work using Google Drive:

- Install the Google Docs Offline extension.
- Access Google Drive's settings.
- Mark the "Offline" checkbox.

Once offline access is established, you can view and edit files, including Google Docs, Google Sheets, and Google Slides, even without internet connectivity. However, for collaborative efforts, internet connectivity remains necessary.

- **Collaborative Sharing:** Sharing files from Google Drive is excellent for cooperative efforts and maintaining shared understanding. Sharing files via Google Drive is a straightforward process, be it a spreadsheet, presentation, document, or any other file type.

  For those new to Google Drive, here's a concise guide on file sharing:

  - Open Google Drive in your browser and select the desired file. Click the "Share" button located in the upper-right corner. A dialogue box will emerge, presenting various options.
  - In the "People with access" section, input the email addresses of individuals you wish to share the file with. Furthermore, you can include a personalized message in the invitation. Should you want recipients to view, edit, or comment on the file, you can use the dropdown menu to specify their level of access.

- If you intend to distribute the file to a sizable audience, you can select the "copy link" option located at the base. It will generate a distinct link allowing anyone to access the file, offering options to view, edit, or provide comments.
- **Unzip ZIP Files:** For a straightforward and cost-free method to unzip ZIP files within your Google Drive, installing the ZIP Extractor app (add-on) is essential. This robust extractor tool accommodates files in RAR, 7z, and TAR formats, encompassing password-protected files.

  Select the ZIP file from your Google Drive, right-click, and opt for the "Open with" feature. The files will be decompressed, enabling you to preview or store them within your Google Drive.

- **Transition to Google One from Drive:** For enhanced storage space for your Google Drive content, upgrading to Google One is an effective approach. This upgrade presents family-sharing benefits, allowing file sharing with your family members.

  This approach allows family members to access shared files and folders regardless of location. It's also possible to individually upgrade family members, granting each their dedicated storage space.

  To initiate an upgrade, click "Buy storage" in the left pane of Google Drive or visit one.google.com to explore the comprehensive shareable plan.

- **Leveraging Templates:** Google Drive offers an array of templates across all account levels, available for Google Sheets, Docs, and Slides. This collection encompasses diverse templates suitable for various project types.

  To access templates, open the respective tool and select "Template Gallery" or use the search function to locate templates suited to your project. Alternatively, from Google Drive's homepage, click "New," choose the desired file type (slides, docs, or sheets), and then select "From a template" to explore Google Drive's template selection.

  Furthermore, Google Forms templates expedite the creation of event invitations and surveys. Visit Google Forms and peruse the template gallery to select options like Contact Information, RSVP, Party Invite, Event Registration, and more.

- **Arranging Files by Size:** By default, Google Drive organizes your uploaded files and folders based on recent additions or modifications, facilitating quick access to frequently used files.

  However, if you intend to optimize Google Drive storage, sorting files by size can aid in identifying and eliminating infrequently used files that consume excessive space.

  Follow these steps:

- Navigate to Google Drive and click "Storage" at the bottom of the left-hand menu.
- It will present a list of files ordered by size, with the largest files appearing first. Remove unnecessary files by clicking the Trash Bin icon.
- Ensure to permanently delete the file from the Trash folder to free up cloud storage space.

- **Engaging in Advanced Search:** You may seek a document containing keywords that appear across numerous files. For this scenario, the advanced search feature within Google Drive proves beneficial. This platform empowers you to refine search outcomes by location, file type, owner, shared recipients, modification date, and other attributes.

  To utilize this feature, click the "Search Options" icon at the rightmost side of the search bar.

Reasons for Using Google Drive

Utilizing Google Drive brings forth numerous advantages, both personally and professionally. Transferring your files to a cloud-based storage system eliminates the need to carry your computer along constantly.

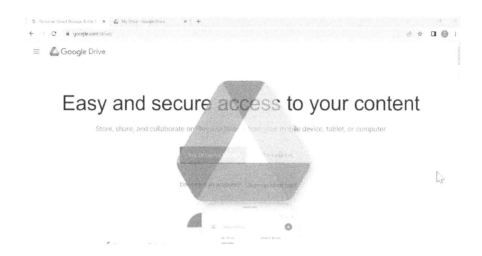

The rationales behind considering Google Drive usage encompass:

- **Mobility:** Accessing your files anywhere is the foremost benefit of storing everything on the cloud. Log into your Google Drive with your Google account on your chosen device. No concerns arise about copying files to USB drives or external hard drives.
  This facet proves especially valuable during presentations at meetings. Exercise caution when accessing a public or non-owned Google Drive account and ensure proper log-out.

- **Synchronization:** Synchronization, closely tied to mobility, is facilitated by Google Drive. Documents can be automatically synchronized across different devices via the internet.

Effortlessly upload files from your computer, phone, and other devices to Google Drive through automatic synchronization.

- **Collaboration:** Traditional file sharing involves steps like attaching files to emails using conventional software. Google's G Suite apps fully leverage the impressive collaboration feature. Google apps streamline and enhance the collaborative process.
Google Drive enables multifaceted collaborations, saving time and potential costs compared to traditional internet systems. It offers a convenient avenue to store company files and foster team collaboration.

- **Intuitive Interface:** Google Drive boasts a user-friendly and intuitive interface, making its usage straightforward. Even if you are still determining the purpose of a specific button, you can hover over it to reveal its name onscreen before clicking.
The interface's simplicity allows easy navigation, ensuring a smooth user experience.

Ways of Using Google Drive

The two ways of accessing Google Drive are via synchronization by using your PC to download the applications and the website via a web customer. Note that you will need a Google account for the two choices you are going for.

It is feasible to get an app for Google Drive installed on your PC, but accessing your files via the app is something a few people may need to be made aware of. They have been referred to as Backup and Sync, as that is the primary purpose of the Google Drive application.

To enable you to download the Google Drive application, log into your account, and afterward, on the right side of the screen, you will see the superior menu; click on it. Select the "Settings" option and the "Get Drive for Desktop" option afterward.

You can also use google.com/drive/download/ to get direct access to the Google Drive application and download it. You can likewise access links for downloading it for Android or iOS via this page.

How your Google storage works

Every Google Account comes with 15 GB of storage divided among Gmail, Google Drive, and Google Photos. If you need more storage, you can buy a Google One subscription, where it's offered. Sometimes, you might receive extra storage through special promotions or associated purchases. For further details about your storage allocation, consult on what items are included in your storage usage.

What counts against your storage quota

- Photos and videos are stored in original quality and backed up on Google Photos.
- Photos and videos stored in high quality (now called Storage Saver) and Express quality backed up on Google Photos after June 1, 2021. Any media backed up

in high quality or Express quality before June 1, 2021, won't be considered for your Google Account storage. Find out more about this modification.

- Emails and attachments within Gmail include items in your Spam and Trash folders.
- Files saved in Google Drive, encompassing PDFs, images, and videos.
- Recordings of Google Meet calls.
- Files generated or edited within collaborative content tools like Google Docs, Sheets, Slides, Drawings, Forms, Recorder, and Jamboard.
- Files generated or modified on or after June 1, 2021, contribute to your usage limit.
- Files that were uploaded or last edited before June 1, 2021, do not factor into your usage limit.

What happens when you're over quota

Exceeding your allocated storage capacity indicates you've utilized more storage space than what's available. If you surpass your storage quota:

- Uploading fresh files or images to Google Drive becomes unavailable.
- Backing up photos and videos to Google Photos is not possible.
- Your ability to send and receive Gmail emails may be affected.
- Generating new files in collaborative content tools like Google Docs, Sheets, Slides, Drawings, Forms, and

Jamboard becomes restricted. Others can only edit or duplicate the impacted files once you decrease storage usage.

- Creating backups for new Recorder files is prohibited.
- Please note: You can still log in and access your Google Account.

If your storage usage remains above the quota for two years or more: If you don't free up space or acquire additional storage to bring your usage below the quota, all your content in Gmail, Google Photos, and Google Drive (including files from Google Docs, Sheets, Slides, Drawings, Forms, and Jamboard) could be deleted.

Before any deletion occurs, we will:

- Notify you through emails and notifications within Google products. We'll contact you at least three months before the content becomes eligible for removal.
- Provide you with the option to prevent deletion (by purchasing extra storage or removing files).
- Allow you the opportunity to download your content from our services. You can find out more about how to download your Google data.

How to go back under quota

Our services offer tools for managing storage, and assisting in recognizing methods to clear storage capacity. An alternative approach involves transferring files to your device for downloading and removal from cloud storage. Consider upgrading to a bigger Google One storage plan to expand Gmail, Drive, and Photos storage.

Advantages and Disadvantages of Google Drive

You can save all your files within a Google Drive, functioning as a secure server for storing your data. Whether individuals or collaborative teams need to manage files for shared projects, Google Drive is the ideal solution.

The Advantages of Google Drive

Google Drive enables you to store your files on their server, granting you access to them as long as you're connected to the internet.

- **Making Adjustments to the Files by Editing:** Google Drive allows continuous access to Google Docs, a platform equipped with editing tools to modify and refine your files. You can consistently access Google Drive and your files if you have a connected device. It's accessible across various devices, such as computers, Macs, iPhones, iPads, and Android.
- **Your File Search Made Effortless:** Google Drive is recognized for facilitating file searches using keywords and file type filters. You can swiftly retrieve your files and search within image files for specific words, even if they're primarily image-based.

- **Versatile File Viewing:** You can seamlessly access any file using Google Drive. The browser supports nearly 30 file formats, eliminating the necessity of local installations or ownership on your computer, which is the optimal approach.
- **Effortless File Sharing with Contacts:** The functionality within Google Drive streamlines sharing files with friends and family, requiring just a few clicks. Depending on your permission settings, your acquaintances can view, edit, or provide comments on your document.
- **Feature-rich:** Google Drive boasts an array of features that establish it as a remarkably versatile choice among cloud storage solutions. Its integration with other Google offerings like Gmail and Google Docs is particularly beneficial. This integration empowers you to collaboratively craft, modify, and engage with documents in real time—a highly advantageous facet for professional or academic projects.

  For instance, a user crafting a presentation using Google Slides can effortlessly incorporate images and videos stored within their Google Drive account. Further capabilities encompass the ability to form unlimited folders and subfolders, share files and folders with others, and access recently opened files offline.

- **Seamless Integration with Google Services:** Google Drive seamlessly melds with well-known Google services such as Docs, Sheets, and Slides. This seamless integration permits direct creation, editing, and teamwork on documents, spreadsheets, and presentations within the confines of Google Drive. Such an integrated environment heightens productivity and simplifies workflow processes.

Moreover, modifications performed in Google Docs, Sheets, or Slides are automatically preserved in Google Drive, ensuring your files remain current.

- **Facilitating Open Dialogues:** This interaction can be facilitated by inserting remarks directly into the files. If your intention involves soliciting feedback and enhancing file collaboration, you can create and respond to specific comments.

- **Automated Backup and Synchronization:** Bid farewell to concerns about file loss due to computer crashes or accidental deletions. Google Drive furnishes automated backup and synchronization functionalities, guaranteeing the security of your files within the cloud and their swift accessibility whenever the need arises. The synchronization capability keeps your files harmonized across all your devices, guaranteeing that you consistently possess the latest iteration.

  Did you know? With Google Drive's automated backup and syncing, your files remain safeguarded, even if your device experiences an unfortunate mishap.

- **Free 15GB and affordable upgrades:** Google Drive provides users with 15 GB of complimentary storage, which is generally sufficient for most individuals' requirements. Should you require more space, an option is to subscribe to Google One. This subscription service grants users access to extra storage for their Google accounts.

For a monthly fee of $1.99, subscribers receive 100 GB of storage across Google Drive, Gmail, and Google Photos. It proves advantageous for those who frequently face storage shortages. Moreover, Google One members enjoy exclusive perks like 24/7 customer support and discounts on select Google products.

- **Diverse file format support:** While Google Drive is often associated with online file storage, it's worth noting that it can open and convert approximately 30 different file formats. These formats encompass those used in Microsoft Office, Photoshop, and various commonly employed software. In essence, Google Drive is more than just storage – it is a versatile virtual office suite.

Disadvantages of Google Drive

Google Drive serves as an impressive tool for file storage, offering numerous benefits, yet it also has its downsides.

- **Security Threats and Data Loss:** One drawback that might be associated with Google Drive involves the risk of hackers infiltrating or deleting your vital data, potentially introducing viruses to your system's server. In such cases, your documents could be wiped out. Especially concerning are sensitive documents like financial summaries or shared files that could become compromised if successfully accessed by hackers.

Undoubtedly, Google employs strong security measures, likely equipped with an exceptional antivirus or security system to safeguard files. However, unforeseen incidents can occur.

- **Limited Offline Usage:** Google Drive's primary focus is online access, which means accessing files offline can be restricted. While certain files and folders can be accessed offline after enabling the feature, offline capabilities may only match the online experience partially, and specific functionalities might be available with an internet connection.

- **Control and Ownership of Files:** Upon uploading files to Google Drive, you grant Google specific rights and permissions in line with their terms of service. This allows Google to analyze and process your files to offer personalized services. While this can enhance user experience, it's essential to comprehend the level of control and ownership you retain over your files while using Google Drive.

- **Storage Constraints:** Although Google Drive provides a generous 15 GB of free storage, individuals with substantial files or those needing more space might have to purchase a storage plan. This could lead to ongoing expenses based on your storage needs. When selecting Google Drive as your primary cloud storage solution, it's vital to factor in your storage requirements and associated costs.

- **Possible Compatibility Challenges:** While Google Drive supports various file formats, certain file types or advanced features of specific applications might need more support. This could result in compatibility problems when opening or editing files within Google Drive. Confirming file type compatibility and necessary functionalities is prudent before relying heavily on Google Drive for specific tasks.

- **Dependency on Google Account:** To utilize Google Drive, possession of a Google Account is essential. However, this heavy reliance on a solitary account could be unfavorable for those who opt to distribute their online presence across various platforms or hold reservations regarding centralized account administration.

  For individuals who wish to maintain the segregation of their online engagements or circumvent the creation of yet another account, the dependence on a Google Account might pose a disadvantage.

- **Upload and Download Speed:** A drawback of Google Drive is its upload and download speed. The speed will likely decelerate when many users attempt to utilize the service simultaneously.

CHAPTER 2: JUMPING RIGHT IN

How to Install the Google Drive App

Select Personal or Business applications, then click the Download button. Agreeing to their Terms of Service before initiating the download is essential. To begin the installation process, tap on the install button; remember that it will take around 2 to 3 minutes to finish.

Once the installation is complete, the configuration page will become visible. Your first step is to log in to your Google+ account. You can log into the app directly or through your web browser.

The second step involves designating the folders you want your Drive to back up, which may include photos and videos. You have the flexibility to determine the size these files will have after uploading, considering options like High quality or Low quality. Additionally, you can choose to upload your photos and videos to Google Photos.

The third and final step involves configuring the Drive folder on your computer. You can opt to synchronize your Google Drive with your PC based on your preference. Synchronizing on your computer is recommended, allowing you to modify the folder locations.

Furthermore, you can synchronize all documents on your computer if you need clarification about potential mix-ups. If you don't plan on mixing up the files, stick with the last step.

Inspect your notification bar adjacent to the clock; an upward-pointing arrow will accompany a novel cloud icon. If you tap this icon, you'll be presented with synchronized files. Furthermore, you can establish shortcuts that lead to the Drive on your default browser, granting access to the Google Drive folder on your computer.

If you manage Backup and Sync through Google, click the three dots. This action permits you to modify preferences, pause synchronization, incorporate a new account, or terminate the application during the process.

Within the preferences, you can manipulate the available space on your Drive by adjusting proxy settings and bandwidth settings for both uploading and downloading operations.

Google Drive Pricing

Regarding storage, you receive a complimentary allocation of 15GB distributed among Drive, Gmail, and Photos. It is generally sufficient for most individuals, although you can increase it by opting for a monthly or yearly subscription, a component of Google One. Subscribing expands your storage and offers additional perks, such as discounts in the Google Store and the ability to share storage with family members.

Narrowing our focus to Google Drive pricing, let's delve into the primary storage options. A 100GB plan comes at a monthly cost of $1.99, the 200GB plan is priced at $2.99 per month, and the most extensive 2TB plan is available for $9.99 monthly. Notably, you can economize by opting for annual payments, which translates to approximately two months of free service on each plan, compared to a month-to-month subscription.

A crucial detail to remember is that Google Photos storage now contributes to your Drive storage limit. If you intend to utilize Photos (a common choice among most Android users), this is a compelling reason to consider upgrading to a paid plan.

How to Sign up for an Account

To utilize Google Drive, owning a Google account is a requisite, and obtaining one is cost-free with a straightforward sign-up procedure facilitated by a stable internet connection. To establish a Google account, you must provide specific information, including your name, birth date, and location. Creating a Google account also grants you access to a complimentary Gmail address and a Google+ profile.

If you already possess a Gmail address, this inherently implies that you already possess a Google account, obviating the need to log into your Drive with your Gmail credentials.

Here's a step-by-step guide to creating your Google account:

- Navigate to www.google.com using your web browser.
- Locate the Sign-in option situated at the upper-right corner of the page.
- Find and select the "Create an account" option.
- A page will appear, prompting you to input your details.
- Include your phone number, which will be used to receive a verification code from Google.

- Enter the received code into the designated box to finalize the process.
- Review and agree to Google's terms and conditions.
- Step 4 involves verifying your account, while Step 5 concludes the account setup process.

Types of Supported Files

While storage capacity stands as a primary concern for the majority of cloud storage solutions, it's worth noting that file type restrictions can also carry significance for numerous users. Fortunately, Google Drive boasts support for many file formats, encompassing .jpeg, .png, .gif, mpeg4, .mov, and .avi — you can refer to the complete list here.

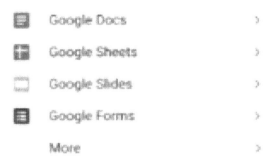

In addition to this, there exist limitations on file sizes, although these limitations are unlikely to pose issues for most users:

- **Documents:** Can comprise up to 1.02 million characters. Conversion of a text document to Google Docs format allows up to 50 MB.

- **Spreadsheets:** Support up to ten million cells or 18,278 columns for sheets created in Google Sheets or converted to it. This limit remains consistent for Excel spreadsheets as well.
- **Presentations:** Conversions to Google Slides permit files of up to 100MB.
- **Google Sites:** Pages can contain up to 15,000,000 characters, with a site maximum of 40,000,000 characters, 10,000 pages, and 15,000 images.
- **All other files:** Up to 5TB is in place.

Additionally, individual users are restricted to uploading 750GB per day. Should a single file exceed 750GB, the user won't be able to upload any more data on that particular day.

Add Drive widget to an iOS Lock Screen

Incorporating the Google Drive widget onto your Lock Screen facilitates direct access to Drive on your iPhone or iPad, eliminating the necessity to unlock your device beforehand.

Key points to consider:

- This functionality is exclusively accessible for iPhones running iOS 16 or newer.
- Widgets can be generated solely for Google apps already installed on your iOS device.

Add & configure a Lock Screen widget.

The Drive app must be installed for the Lock Screen widget to appear in the gallery.

1. To access Customization mode, press and hold the Lock Screen.
2. Choose Customize.
3. Tap the Lock Screen and then Add Widgets.
- Navigate to the Drive widget.
- Tap the Drive widget.
- Drag the widget to the shortcut bar located beneath the clock.
- Once the Drive widget is in the bar, tap it to access settings.
- Pick your desired configuration, select Done, and subsequently Set it as Wallpaper Pair.
- Tap the Lock Screen to exit customization until you're no longer in Customization mode.

Customize a Drive Lock Screen widget.

- Utilize FaceID to unlock the Lock Screen.
- Invoke Customization mode by pressing and holding the Lock Screen.
- Choose Customize.
- Tap the current Drive widget within the widget bar to reveal the Lock Screen widget gallery.
- To access settings, tap the widget once more.
- Select your desired configuration.
- To close the widget gallery, choose the X icon, followed by Done.
- To conclude customization, tap the Lock Screen until you exit Customization mode.

Two-step Verification

Your Drive's security level hinges on your Google account's security, as unauthorized access to your files would be highly undesirable.

- For enhanced security, we're introducing you to "2-step verification," an extra layer of protection for your account. With 2-step verification, confirming access to your account involves an additional confirmation step.
- In the initial phase of this verification process, you must create a robust password by incorporating a combination of upper and lowercase letters, numbers, and a symbol. This will result in a strong password. Subsequently, the second phase acts as an added security measure. It entails receiving a code on your mobile phone, which needs to be in proximity and operational during this process.

How to Use Gmail's Drive Integration

When transferring a Drive file through Gmail, start composing a message and select the Drive icon at the bottom of your screen. It will grant you access to the file's location before initiating the transfer. On an Android device, opt for the Attach feature positioned at the screen's top, then Insert the file from Drive. This process allows you to share substantial files as links instead of attaching them directly.

To save Gmail files to your Drive, hover over the media file and click the Drive icon at the bottom right corner. You'll need to long-press the image on mobile devices, then tap View image. Next, tap the options icon, represented by three dots at the top right, and select Store on Drive.

When it comes to Gmail files, they contribute to a comparable storage limit as Drive files. For example, photos from Google Photos share the same storage limit. This approach streamlines accessibility within the Drive setup, whether using the web, desktop, or Android/iPhone clients. Consequently, you're not conserving any storage space by employing this method.

CHAPTER 3: GOOGLE DRIVE ORIENTATION AND NAVIGATION

Google Drive Navigation

Google Drive on the Web provides the convenience of storing, accessing, and editing your files from various locations: online, on your local hard drive, or while on the move. The following are ways you can utilize Google Drive on the web using a screen reader:

- Download, upload, create, store, and edit files.
- Collaboratively share files and folders with family, friends, classmates, or colleagues.
- Organize files systematically into folders.
- Securely store files, granting you accessibility from any device.
- Upon launching Google Drive, your focus will be directed to the central interface area known as the list view. The initial folder or file in the list will be audibly announced. To navigate through files and folders, utilize the up and down arrow keys. To open an item, press the "o" key or the Enter key.

Google Drive features a range of keyboard shortcuts designed to expedite and simplify navigation. Among the most frequently used shortcuts is the "Go to" action. This function allows you to swiftly shift your focus to specific interface sections by pressing "g" followed by another key. Several common "Go to" actions in Google Drive include:

- **G then N:** To access the navigation pane where you can select how files and folders are displayed. This pane encompasses views like My Drive, Shared with Me, Recent, Starred, and Trash.
- **G then L:** To reach the list of files and folders, the content varies based on your navigation pane selection.
- **G then D:** To access the details pane of a chosen item, offering information like the owner, file size, and last modification date.
- **G then T:** To navigate to top buttons and menus, facilitating actions such as creating new files or folders and sorting the list view.

Keyboard shortcuts

For swift navigation within Drive, you can employ Drive's keyboard shortcuts.

- To access a compilation of shortcuts in Drive, press Ctrl + / (forward slash) for Windows or Chrome OS, and ⌘ + / (forward slash) for Mac.

Search for files

For conducting searches within Drive:

- Access the Search box by pressing / (forward slash).

- Enter your search terms, and then hit Enter. The focus will shift to the files and folders corresponding to your search terms.
- Utilize the arrow keys to navigate through the search results.

For performing an advanced search:

- Reach the Search box by pressing / (forward slash).
- Move to the Search options menu by pressing Tab, then press Enter.
- Use the menus and text fields within the search options dialogue to refine your search.
- Navigate to the Search button, then press Enter. The focus will transition to the list of files and folders matching your search terms.
- Navigate through the search results using the arrow keys.
- For further insights and recommendations on using the Search box in Drive, refer to the "Search for your files" section. To locate or recover deleted files, learn the process in the "Find or recover a file" section.

Sort files

For organizing your files:

- Tap the "r" key to access the Sort menu.
- Utilize the down or up arrow keys to navigate within the menu. Pay attention to whether options like "Name" and

"Last modified" are marked as "checked" or "not checked."

- To choose a sorting option, press Enter. Your attention will be redirected to the list of files and folders.

Top-level buttons and menus

The Google Drive interface features a variety of buttons and menus that allow you to execute different tasks on your files and folders. Many of these buttons come with keyboard shortcuts for swift access, and you can also use Tab and Shift + Tab to navigate between them.

Here's a compilation of Google Drive buttons and menus accessible at all times:

- **Create:** Press "c." Utilize this menu to generate a new folder or file.
- **Folder actions:** Press "F." This menu lets you take actions on the presently displayed folder.
- **Grid or list view:** Press "V." By pressing this button, you can alternate between viewing items in list or grid format.
- **Sort:** Press "R." Use this menu to arrange items.
- **Details:** Press "D." This button expands or collapses the details pane.
- **Settings:** Press "T." You can modify your Drive settings or navigate to Help information via this menu.

When you've selected a file or folder, the subsequent buttons and menus become available:

- **More actions:** Press "a" to open this menu, offering a range of available actions for the chosen item.
- **Share:** Press "." (period) to access the Sharing settings for the file or folder.
- **Move:** Press "Z" to relocate items to a designated folder.
- **Remove:** Press "#" (pound) to transfer an item to the Trash.

Views

A view in Google Drive signifies a method of presenting the content. Each view encompasses the files and folders pertinent to that particular view. Google Drive offers the following views:

- My Drive includes all the folders and items you've created or uploaded within Google Drive.
- Shared with Me displays files and folders that have been shared with you.
- Starred showcases items you've marked with a star.
- Recent exhibit items you've accessed recently.
- Trash contains everything you've deleted. If you move an item to Trash, you can restore it by relocating it to My Drive.

To alter your Google Drive view, follow these instructions:

- Press "G" followed by "N" to direct focus to the navigation panel.
- Employ the down or up arrow to navigate through the views and folders. If a folder contains sub-folders, use

the right arrow to expand it. Continue using the up and down arrows to explore sub-folders.

- Once you've chosen the desired view or folder to navigate, press Enter to select that view, shifting focus to the list of items within it.
- At this point, you can navigate the list using the down or up arrow.

A few additional points regarding Google Drive views:

- A file or folder can appear in multiple views. For example, a document you starred and recently opened will be visible in both the Starred and Recent views.
- Within each view, items can be presented as a grid or a list. To switch between grid and list view, press "V."
- While traversing Google Drive, your screen reader provides you with details concerning selected folders and files.
- Within the navigation pane, you'll be informed about the folder's name along with the label "Google Drive folder." This includes whether the folder is currently selected and its position in the list (e.g., "two of five"). For folders containing sub-folders, your screen reader will indicate whether they're collapsed or expanded.
- In the list view, you'll receive auditory information about the name of the file or folder, the owner, the latest modifier, and the date of the most recent modification.

CHAPTER 4: WORKING WITH GOOGLE DRIVE

How to Create Folders in Google Drive

For computer:

1. Visit drive.google.com using your computer.
2. Towards the left, select New and then opt for the folder choice.

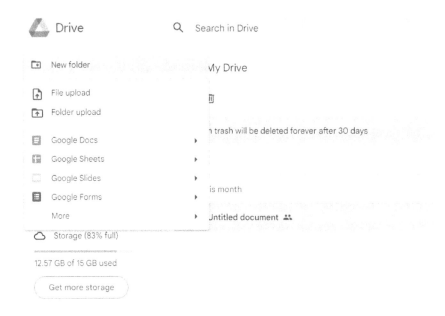

3. Assign a name to your folder.

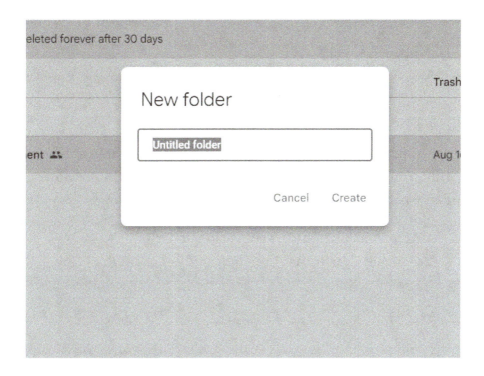

4. Click on Create.

For Android:

1. Launch the Google Drive app on your Android device.
2. Tap the "Add" button located at the bottom right.
3. Select "Folder."
4. Provide a name for the folder.
5. Tap on Create.

For iPhone and iPad:

1. Make sure to open the Google Drive app on your iPhone or iPad.
2. Tap the "Add" button, positioned at the bottom right.
3. Choose "Folder."

4. Enter a name for the folder.

5. Select Create.

Change owners in Google Drive

You can shift the ownership of a file to an individual with whom you've previously shared the file, but this is feasible solely on your computer. The process cannot be executed on Android, iPad, or iPhone devices.

1. On your computer, access Google Drive.

2. Locate the desired file, then right-click on it.

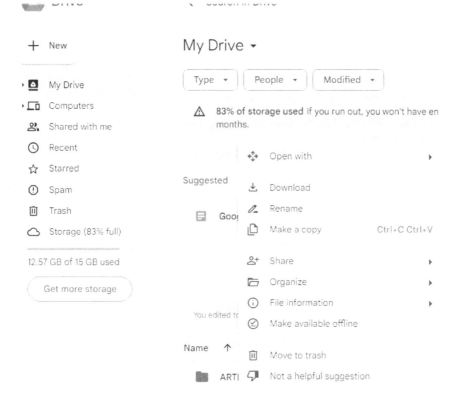

3. Choose Share > Share from the ensuing menu.

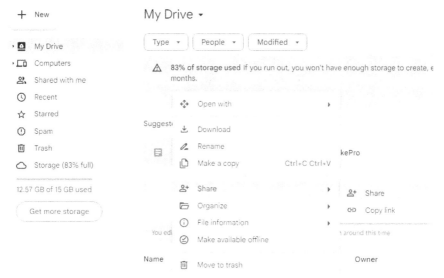

4. Adjacent to the recipient's name, click the downward arrow, and subsequently select Transfer ownership.

Manage files in Google Drive with a screen reader

Create a new file or folder

For generating fresh content within Drive, utilize the following keyboard shortcuts. A new, untitled file will launch in a separate tab.

- Shift + t: Initiate a new text document.
- Shift + p: Commence a new presentation.
- Shift + s: Begin a new spreadsheet.
  Shift + d: Launch a new drawing.

- Shift + o: Start a new form.

- To generate a novel folder, utilize Shift + f. This action triggers the New folder dialog, positioning your cursor within the text field. After entering a new folder name, press Enter. Your focus will revert to the Drive list view, with the newly created folder highlighted.
- As an alternative to the keyboard above shortcuts, press "c" to open the New menu. Progress through the menu using the down arrow, then select an option by pressing Enter.

Share a file or folder

It's possible to grant others access to view, comment on, or edit files or folders.

- To access the sharing settings for a chosen file or folder, press the "." (dot) key.
- To determine the visibility level for your file or folder, navigate to "Stop, limit, or change sharing." The options differ depending on whether your item was created within a domain and the sharing regulations established by your administrator.

Move a file or folder

To relocate files into folders or place folders within other folders, adhere to these guidelines:

- To focus on the list of items, use the shortcut g followed by l.

- To designate a file or folder, navigate with the arrow keys. To select multiple items, hold Shift while using the arrow keys.
- Access the Move dialog by pressing z.
- Use the arrow keys to pick a destination folder.
- Once positioned on the Move button, press Enter.
- Exiting the dialog might necessitate pressing Escape.

For transferring a file or folder to the trash, proceed as follows:

- Within a list of files and folders, choose one or more items for deletion.
- Press # to initiate removal.
- Items owned by you will be moved to the trash upon removal. If you remove an item that you don't own, it will be deleted from your Drive but will remain in others' Drives. Refer to further information about deleting and restoring files.

Upload and download files

To add files or folders to Drive, proceed as follows:

- Press "c" to unveil the New menu.
- Choose either File upload or Folder upload.
- Select the desired file or folder for upload, and press Enter.

To retrieve a file or folder from Google Drive, adhere to these instructions:

- Select the file you wish to download.

- Press "a" to access the Actions menu.
- Opt for Download.

Make a copy of a file

To duplicate a file, adhere to these guidelines:

- Within a list of files and folders, designate the desired file for duplication.
- Press "a" to unveil the Actions menu.
- Opt for "Make a copy."
- A replica of the item will be generated in My Drive, denoted as "Copy of" followed by the original title.

How to Upload and Download Files

Before accessing your files on Google Drive, it's necessary to upload them through the web, PC, or mobile client. Let's begin by discussing the web version, which offers two methods for uploading files to Drive.

Upload to Google Drive using a browser

There are two ways to upload files to Drive. The first method involves dragging and dropping the desired file or folder from your PC onto the Drive in your browser. An upload progress window will appear at the bottom right.

The second option requires clicking the New button in the website's top-left corner and selecting File Upload or Folder Upload. After choosing the items you wish to upload, click Open or Upload and wait for the process to finish. Here's a step-by-step guide:

1. Open your browser and navigate to the Google Drive website.
2. Click on the New button located at the top-left corner.

3. Choose either File upload or Folder upload.

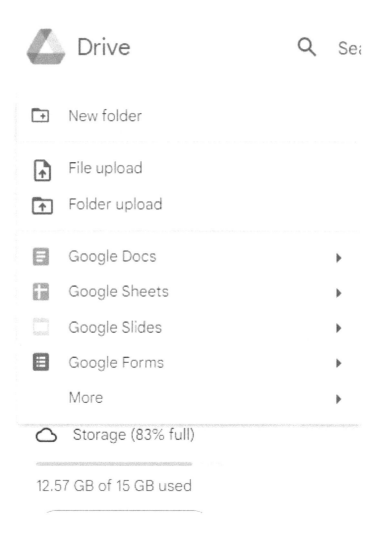

4. Select the files or folders you want to upload.
5. Click Open or Upload to start the upload process.

Upload to Google Drive using the desktop client

A more straightforward way to upload to Google's cloud server is using Google Drive for Desktop. This application generates synchronized Google Drive folders on your PC. You can easily upload documents by dragging and dropping them into the Drive folder. This process is similar to moving files between folders on your computer, but there might be a delay as the files synchronize.

Upload to Google Drive using your smartphone

Transferring files from your mobile device is just as convenient. Launch the Drive app, click the + symbol in the lower-right corner, choose Upload, and pick the file you wish to transfer to the cloud. Alternatively, you can rapidly upload files by opening them, pressing the Share button, and selecting Drive.

Here are the step-by-step directions:

1. Open the Drive app on your smartphone.
2. Click the + icon.

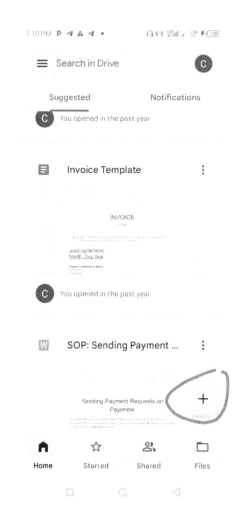

3. Choose Upload.

4. Tap the files you want to upload.

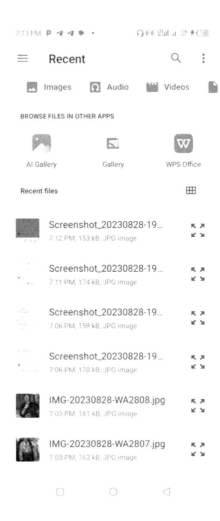

Downloading files using a browser.

Retrieving files from Google Drive is quick and straightforward on any internet-connected device. If you're utilizing Google Drive for Desktop, anything you upload can be duplicated to any folder on your computer, similar to regular files. Additionally, you can download files from the web client by right-clicking and choosing the Download option. This method applies to both single files and entire folders.

Downloading files using the smartphone app

Leaving your files in the cloud and accessing them when necessary can be more convenient on mobile devices. However, certain scenarios may require you to locate the Google Drive download option. To do so, locate your file within the Drive app, tap the three-dot menu icon on the right, choose Download, and you're all set.

Here's a breakdown of the steps:

1. Open the Drive app on your smartphone.
2. Locate the desired file. Tap the three-dot menu icon beside it.

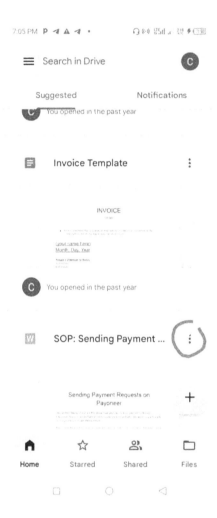

3. Opt for the Download option.

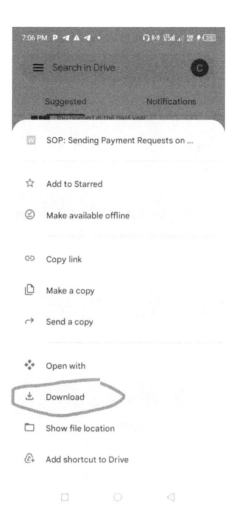

How to Organize and Delete Files on Google Drive

You can structure your Drive files just as you would on your computer. You can either keep them in a single location (typically My Drive) or categorize them into various folders and subfolders. Regardless of your chosen organization method, you can easily search for your files using the search bar at the top of the screen.

Creating a new folder on the web

Creating a folder within the web client involves clicking the New button and opting for the New folder. Similarly, on your computer's Drive folder, you can create a new folder by right-clicking, just as you would in Windows. On mobile devices, tap the blue + button and select Folder.

Here's a step-by-step guide:

1. Visit the Google Drive website on your computer.
2. Click the New button and choose New folder.

3. Alternatively, right-click anywhere and select New folder.
4. Provide a name for the folder and click Create.

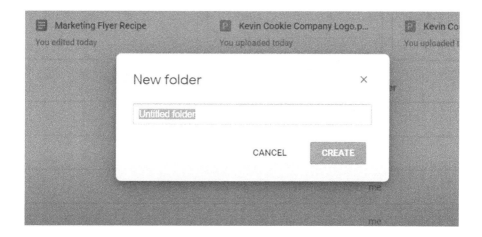

Moving files on the web

When it comes to moving files in the web client, you can use the drag-and-drop method for both the web interface and the Drive folder. You can also right-click a file, choose Move To, navigate to the desired destination, and select Move Here.

Follow these steps:

1. Access the Google Drive website on your computer.
2. Right-click the file you wish to move.

3. Select Move To.

4. Navigate to the target folder.
5. Confirm the move.

Moving files on the mobile app

For moving files using the mobile app, although drag-and-drop is feasible, I've found that it's more efficient to tap the More actions icon (three vertical dots) adjacent to a file, pick the Move option, and then select the new file location.

Follow these steps:

1. Drag and drop files for movement.
2. Alternatively, open the mobile Drive app.
3. Locate the file you want to move and tap the three-dot icon.
4. Opt for Move.
5. Navigate to the new location and confirm with Move.

How to delete Drive files on the web

As cloud storage is limited, it's crucial to understand how to remove Drive files to free up space. The simplest approach on the web is to right-click on the file or folder and choose the Remove option.

Here's how to do it step by step:

1. Launch the Google Drive app on your phone.
2. Locate the file you intend to delete. Tap the three-dot menu icon adjacent to it.

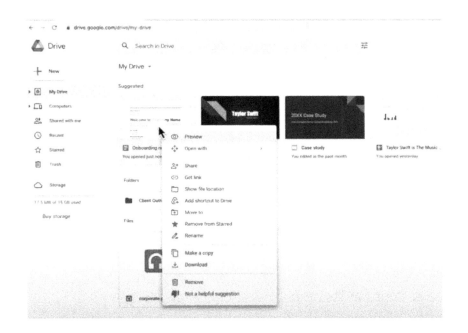

3. Click Remove.

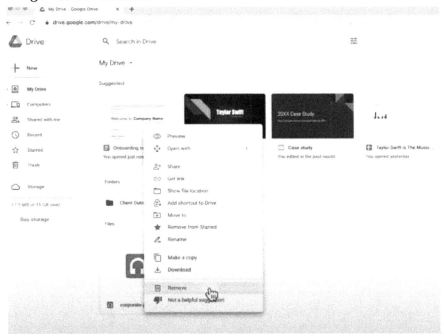

4. Choose Move to trash.

How to delete Drive files on the mobile app

For erasing a Drive document from your mobile device, tap the More actions icon (three vertical dots) beside the file and choose Remove. Then, confirm the action by selecting Move to trash.

Here's how to do it step by step:

1. Launch the Google Drive app on your phone.
2. Locate the file you intend to delete. Tap the three-dot menu icon adjacent to it.

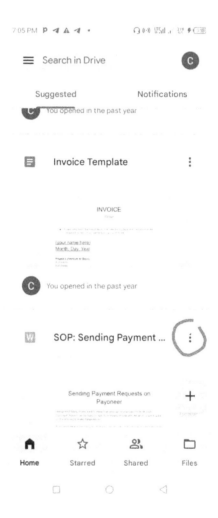

3. Click Remove.
4. Choose Move to trash.

Restore files you deleted

If you've erased an item in the near past using either Google Drive or the Google Drive desktop application, there's a possibility that you can personally recover the file..

Restore from your Trash

Navigate to drive.google.com/drive/trash using a computer. A helpful tip is to arrange your trashed files by the date they were trashed, allowing you to locate the oldest or most recent ones. Right-click on the desired file you wish to retrieve, then select the "Restore" option. Your restored files will appear in their initial location. In case the original location is no longer available, check within the "My Drive" section.

Find a file you don't think you deleted

Check the activity panel
1. Go to drive.google.com on your computer.
2. At the top right, click Info.
3. To check the activity panel Click on "Activity."
4. Look for your file.

Use an advanced search

1. Go to drive.google.com, on your computer.
2. Click the icon to the far right.
3. To find your file, make use of the advanced search options. For example, see spreadsheets, next to 'Type,' click the down arrow, then click 'Spreadsheets.'

Why files go missing

If you cannot locate a file you made in Drive, the folder it was stored in may have been misplaced. The file is still present, but locating it might be more challenging.

How files lose their folder

If you generate a file within another person's folder and erase that particular folder, the file remains unaffected. Instead, it's automatically transferred to your My Drive. It's crucial to note that you can only eliminate files under your ownership. Similarly, when you distribute a folder with someone, and they eliminate your file, the file endures, automatically relocating to your My Drive.

Find unorganized files

Open up drive.google.com on your computer. Utilize the search bar to type: is:unorganized owner:me. Once you locate the file, shift it to a folder within My Drive. This will enhance its accessibility for future reference.

How to use the spam folder in Google Drive

The Google Drive spam folder is a new addition to the online storage space. As its name suggests, users can move any unwanted documents shared with you without your permission. Any file moved to the spam folder will also be removed from your drive after 30 days. Within that time, you won't receive any updates on the file, nor will you be able to interact with it. Notably, files that Google suspects could be spam will be moved to this folder, but users can manually move any file to this folder. In this sense, it functions similarly to the Gmail spam folder.

How to manually move files to the spam folder

You have the ability to relocate any file to the spam folder by simply dragging and dropping it within Google Drive.

To achieve this on your computer:

- Access drive.google.com using a web browser and press Enter.
- Click on "Go to Drive."
- Log in with your Google credentials.
- Locate the desired file, then drag and drop it into the Spam folder on the left-hand sidebar.
- A popup labeled "What are you reporting?" will appear. Choose one of the five content-related options.
- You can also opt to block the sender of the file.

Performing this task on a desktop is notably easier than on Android. However, if you wish to mark a file as spam on your phone:

- Open Google Drive.
- Locate the file, then tap the three-button menu icon.
- Select "Report."
- Choose either "Spam" or "Fraud."
- You can also decide to block the sender or owner of the file.
- Please note, it's not feasible to move entire folders as spam, but you can report folders to Google.

Removing files from the spam folder

To permanently delete a file from the spam folder:

- Open the Spam folder.
- Find the file you want to delete and select the three-button menu icon.
- Choose "Permanently delete."
- To remove all files from the Spam folder, select "Remove all spam files now" at the top of the spam folder.

How to Share Files on Google

Sharing files on the web

An exceptional aspect of Drive involves the capability to collaborate by sharing files. It encompasses individual documents as well as entire folders. To share a Google Drive file or folder, perform the following steps:

1. Right-click on the item.
2. Opt for the Share feature.
3. Adjust the settings according to your preferences.
4. Select the Copy link to distribute the link to your desired recipients.

It's essential to recognize that you possess a degree of control over the privileges associated with your link. The default mode, Restricted, ensures that only individuals you invite can access the file. You can modify this setting, granting "Anyone with the link" the ability to view, comment, or edit.

For a step-by-step guide:

1. Open the Google Drive website on your computer.
2. Right-click the file you intend to share.

3. Choose the Share option.

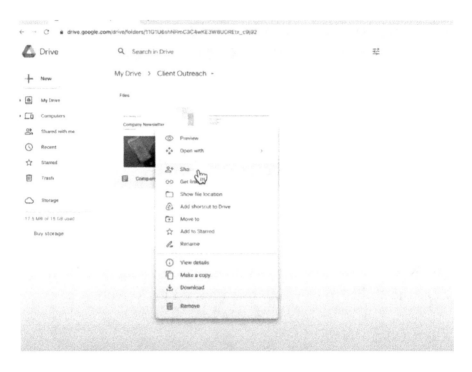

4. Customize the preferences to suit your requirements.

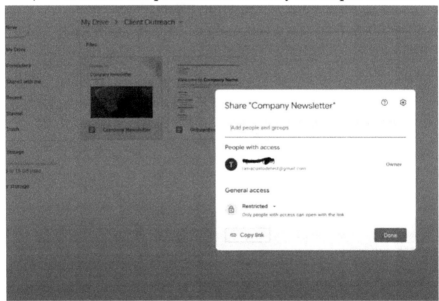

5. Click on the Copy link.
6. Distribute the link to your chosen recipients.

Sharing files on the mobile app

The procedure remains comparable when using mobile devices. You can oversee sharing settings by tapping the More actions icon (represented by three vertical dots) adjacent to a file and then choosing Manage access. Tapping the chain icon enables you to duplicate the link, which can be shared with anyone. Alternatively, you can tap Add People to forward the link to an email address.

Here's a step-by-step guide:

1. Launch the Drive app on your smartphone or tablet.
2. Locate the specific file or folder intended for sharing.
3. Tap the three-dot menu button situated beside it.

4. Select Manage access.

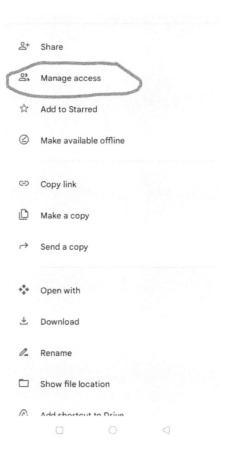

5. Adjust the settings to your preferences.

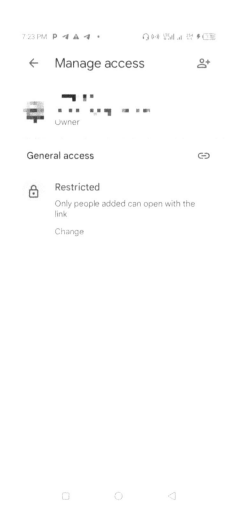

6. Tap the chain link icon to copy the link.

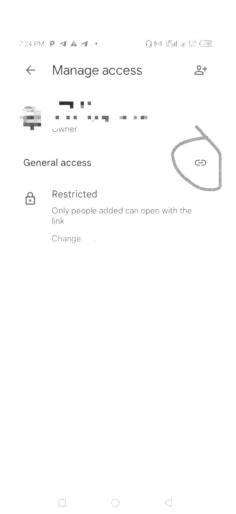

Distribute the link to your chosen recipients.

Stop sharing a file or folder

- Locate the file or folder within Google Drive, Google Docs, Google Sheets, or Google Slides.
- Access or choose the specific file or folder.
- Click on Share or Share Share.

- Identify the individual from whom you wish to revoke sharing permissions.
- Beside their name, click on the Down arrow, and then select Remove access.
- Lastly, click on Save.

Restrict general access for a file or folder

By altering the overall accessibility of an item to Restricted, only individuals with authorized access will be able to open the file.

Here's how you can do it:

1. Locate the file or folder within Google Drive, Google Docs, Google Sheets, or Google Slides.
2. Open or choose the specific file or folder.
3. Click on Share Share or Share Share, then choose Copy link
4. Beneath the "General access" section, click the Down arrow.
5. Opt for Restricted.
6. Click Done.

Delete a shared file

If you remove a shared file you possess:

- Individuals with viewing, commenting, or editing access can generate a copy until the file is entirely erased. To permanently remove the file, access it within your trash and choose Delete forever.

If you erase a shared file you don't possess:

- The file will be taken off your Drive, yet other collaborators can continue to access it. To retrieve the file, open its link, navigate to File, and select Add to My Drive.

Prevent people from downloading, printing, or copying your file

To hinder viewers and commenters from printing, copying, or downloading your file:

- Locate the desired file or folder in Google Drive, Google Docs, Google Sheets, or Google Slides.
- Choose one or more files you wish to impose restrictions on.
- Click on Share or Share Share.
- At the top, access Settings Settings.
- Deselect the option "Viewers and commenters can see the option to download, print, and copy."
- Please be aware that while you can manage sharing, printing, downloading, and copying within Google Drive, Docs, Sheets, and Slides, you cannot prevent others from sharing the file content through other means.

Prevent others from sharing your files

When you're sharing a file, both the owner and individuals with editor privileges retain the ability to modify permissions and share the file. To restrict others from sharing your file:

- Access the file within Google Drive, Google Docs, Google Sheets, or Google Slides.
- Click on Share or Share Share.
- At the top, select Settings Settings.
- Deselect the option "Editors can change permissions and share."

If you prohibit sharing for a folder, this restriction only applies to the folder itself. To prevent the sharing of the files within, you need to adjust this setting individually for each file.

Set an expiration date for a file

- Access a file within Google Drive, Google Docs, Google Sheets, or Google Slides.
- Select the Share option and locate the user to whom you wish to grant temporary permissions.
  If you haven't previously shared the file with that individual, input their email address and press Send or Share. At the top right of the document, select Share again.

- Beside the person's name, click the Down arrow and then select Add expiration.
- Adjacent to "Access expires," choose a date from within the upcoming year to set as the expiration date.

- Click on Save.

How to Use Google Drive Offline

Storing your files in the cloud offers the advantage of accessing them across various devices, but it also implies that you might not have visibility or editing capabilities when offline. Luckily, Google Drive addresses this constraint through an offline mode, enabling you to access files even without an internet connection. This mode lets you view and edit files, encompassing Google Docs, Sheets, and Slides. Any modifications made are automatically synchronized once an internet connection is reestablished.

Using Google Drive offline on the web

To activate offline access, you must individually enable it for each device. When using a browser, access Google Drive, click the gear icon, and access Settings. Toggle on the Offline mode option. Additionally, ensure you download the Google Docs offline Chrome extension. With these steps completed, you can visit the Drive website to view or edit your files. Keep in mind that this process requires the use of the Chrome browser. Alternatively, you can access files through the Drive folder on your computer, which will then open in Chrome.

Here's a step-by-step guide:

1. Visit the Google Drive website.

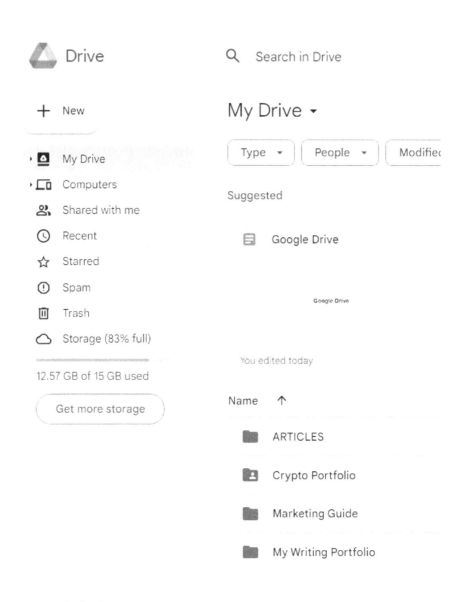

2. Click the Gear icon.

3. Choose Settings.

4. Activate Offline mode by marking the checkbox next to it.

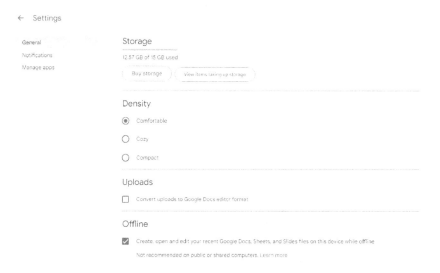

Using Google Drive offline on the mobile app

The process varies slightly when using mobile devices. To enable offline access, open the Drive app, tap the More actions icon (represented by three vertical dots) adjacent to a file, and choose Make available offline. Another option is to long-press on a file and select additional files. Employ the same steps to activate offline mode for multiple files simultaneously.

Here's a step-by-step guide:

1. Launch the Drive app.
2. Locate the desired file you wish to make available offline.
3. Tap the three-dot menu button located beside it.
4. Opt for Make available offline.

Use Dark theme in Google Drive

You can adjust your theme settings for improved file viewing on your mobile device. You can utilize the dark theme option to conserve battery life.

For Android:

- On your Android phone or tablet, launch the Google Drive app.
- Tap the Menu icon located at the top left.
- Select Settings.
- Choose the Theme option.
- Pick between Dark, Light, or System default.

For iPhone and iPad:

- Dark Mode is solely accessible on iOS 13 and later versions.
- Activate Dark Mode on your iPhone or iPad.
- Open the Google Drive app.

How to Create Documents on Google Drive

Using Google Drive, you can generate and modify various types of files, such as documents, spreadsheets, and presentations.

There are five distinct file categories you can produce on Google Drive, each serving a specific purpose:

- **Documents:** Used for crafting letters, flyers, articles, and text-based content.
- **Spreadsheets:** Utilized for organizing and storing information.
- **Presentations:** Designed for creating slideshows.
- **Forms:** Employed to collect and manage data.
- **Drawings:** Used to create simple vector graphics or diagrams.

The process for generating new files is relatively consistent across all file types:

1. Locate and click the "New" button in Google Drive.

2. Select the desired file type.

3. The new file will open in a new browser tab titled "Untitled." It can be found in the upper-left corner of the screen.

4. Rename the file by clicking "OK" in the displayed rename dialog box.

5. Your file is now renamed and saved automatically in Google Drive, accessible anytime.

6. Notably, Google Drive uses autosave, eliminating the need for a manual save button. Edits are automatically saved as you work on the file.

How to Use Google Drive with Third-party Apps

Google Drive is linked with Google's suite of office tools, known as Google Workspace, which includes counterparts to Microsoft's Word, Excel, and PowerPoint, namely Google Docs, Sheets, and Slides. Although these services have dedicated web pages, every document you create is automatically stored within Drive. The drive also provides support for additional Google offerings like Google Forms and Google Drawings.

Creating a document can be initiated directly from Drive's online platform or mobile application, leading you to a dedicated page for that particular Google Doc. How do I go about it? Just click the "New" button in the upper-left corner of the website, and from there, choose Google Docs, Google Sheets, or Google Slides. On a mobile device, tap the blue "+" icon and select one of the three options mentioned earlier.

Here's a step-by-step guide:

- Access the Google Drive website or open the mobile app.
- Click on the "New" button.
- Opt for Google Docs, Google Sheets, or Google Slides.
- Regardless of your selection, all documents created can be conveniently accessed from your computer, mobile device, and the Drive folder on your PC, as long as an internet connection is available.

Furthermore, Google Drive seamlessly integrates with a variety of third-party applications, including:

- DocHub for PDF signatures
- Pixlr Express for photo editing
- Draw.io for diagrams
- and many more.

To explore the complete selection of integrated apps, visit the web interface, click "New," then "More," and finally, "Connect more apps." When you find ad app that interests you, click on it, and select the "Install" button to incorporate it into your Drive experience.

Using Gmail's Drive Integration

One of the most valuable and effective collaborations exists between Gmail and Drive. Interestingly, even before the establishment of Google Drive, enthusiasts had devised an unofficial method to utilize Gmail as a storage solution. It was achieved through a program called Gmail Drive, which enabled Gmail as a storage medium. However, with the introduction of Google Drive and Drive for Desktop, the need for Gmail Drive became obsolete, and consequently, it has yet to be maintained or supported.

Inserting Drive file on Gmail for web

When you want to distribute a Drive file via Gmail, initiate the process by creating a new message and tapping the Drive icon at the lower part of the interface. Subsequently, you can navigate to the desired file and choose the "Insert" option. If you're using a mobile device, access the Attach icon (depicted as a paperclip) at the top of the screen, then select "Insert from Drive." This method is also advantageous for sharing substantial files via links rather than traditional attachments.

Here's a breakdown of the steps:

1. Open Gmail.com.

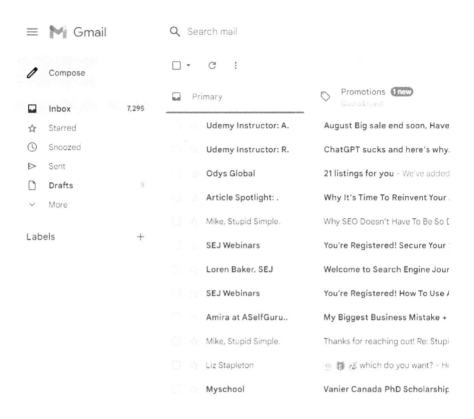

2. Click on "Compose."

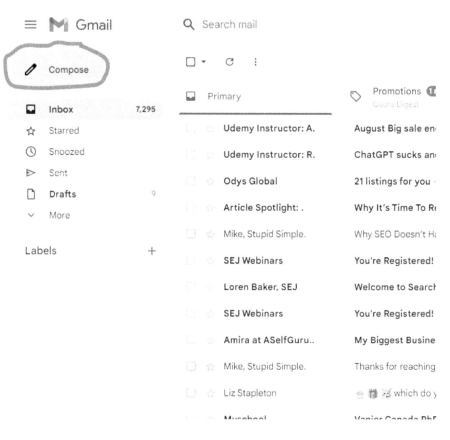

3. Draft your email and fill in all necessary details.
4. Click the Google Drive icon. Locate your file and insert it.

5. Send your email.

Additionally, saving Gmail files to Drive is a straightforward process. Hover the cursor over the attached media file or image and click the "Add to Drive" icon. You'll need to locate the attached file on mobile devices and choose the Drive icon for this action.

Inserting Drive file on Gmail mobile app

1. Launch the Gmail application.
2. Click on the Compose button.

3. Tap the paperclip icon.
4. Choose Insert from Drive.
5. Locate and select the desired file.
6. Send your email.

It's important to mention that files within Gmail contribute to the same storage cap as those stored in Drive (similar to photos uploaded to Google Photos). Therefore, this approach doesn't save you any storage space. Nevertheless, it does enhance the convenience of locating these files within the Drive interface across web, mobile, and desktop platforms.

Collaboration in Google Drive: Everything About Sharing

While the Google Drive platform offers the opportunity to share files and folders, it also provides the capability for others to view or edit them. It is the most optimal choice for groups seeking a seamless solution to exchange files and address this specific concern consistently.

How to Share Files and Folders

It's crucial to comprehend the proper procedure for effectively sharing files and folders in collaborative scenarios, along with understanding the permissions granted to individuals. Below is a straightforward, step-by-step guide outlining how to achieve this:

- Choose the file or folder you wish to share and click the appropriate button. Opt for the "Share" option.

- This is the opportune moment to configure permissions for both folders and files.

For files, three options are available:

- **Can edit:** People can perform various actions, including viewing, editing, printing, and deleting. This provides comprehensive control and document access, which is particularly useful for collaborative document creation.
- **Can comment:** Useful for soliciting input on documents through comments and annotations.
- **Can view:** Individuals can only view the document without engaging in actions such as typing, downloading, copying, printing, or deleting. However, they can create an editable copy of the document.

For folders, two distinct options exist:

- Can organize, add & edit: Individuals possess the authority to edit files, add new ones, and remove existing ones.
- **Can view only:** People are restricted to viewing files, and unable to delete or add new folders/files.
- You can use a link to share the folder or file with specific individuals. Select "Get shareable link," then customize the permissions as desired. Subsequently, you can share the link via email, social media, or any other communication channel. It's important to note that while this method is convenient, it poses security risks, a topic we'll delve into in detail.

Advanced Sharing Options

Within Google Drive, you'll encounter a range of advanced options for sharing files and folders, all closely tied to the security of your stored data.

When you opt to share a file or folder, granting individuals full access might inadvertently lead to their ability to share them with others, posing potential risks and hazards. To address this concern:

- Access the permissions pop-up and select "Advanced."
- Configure the "Prevent editors from changing access" setting to enhance control.
- Modify the setting "Disable options to download, print, and copy for commenters and viewers" to restrict these actions.

In the "Sharing settings" section, those with access permission for the file or folder, apart from the original grant, can be managed under your supervision. Click "Change" to make desired modifications. The pop-up window related to "Link sharing" will emerge, providing advanced sharing choices:

- **Public on the web:** This option allows anyone online to access your file or folder. While powerful, it carries risks, as it might appear in Google searches.
- **Anyone with the link:** All individuals can access the file or folder.
- **On [enterprise]:** This option is restricted to company personnel within Google Suite accounts.

- **Anyone at [enterprise] with the link:** Access is confined to current company members, with the link also applicable for Google Suite accounts.
- **Specific people:** This option enables tailored access, ideal for maintaining limited or private availability. You can select this when necessary to prevent public access.

Expiration dates

At times, it's essential to establish a designated term for an individual, enabling you to access it when sharing files and folders. The expiration date holds significant importance and is a vital setting available in the "Sharing settings" popup. To successfully carry out these actions, follow these steps:

- Open the "Sharing settings" popup and navigate to the "Who has access" section.
- Hover your mouse cursor over the names of the individuals you wish to restrict time-limited access to.
- Once the timer icon labeled "Set expiration" appears, click on it.
- The "Access expires" label will appear above the person's name and email. You can choose between 7 days, 30 days, or a Custom date.
- If you opt for a specific date, select the dropdown box that appears and then click "Save changes."
- Only those granted access to view or comment on a file or folder can utilize this feature. Be cautious, as the individuals' permission to edit will be restricted based on the applied date. Even though you can still obtain the

date when their editing permission takes effect, they will automatically retain viewing capabilities, losing their editing privileges.

CONCLUSION

Google Drive stands out as a robust cloud-based storage and teamwork platform that's revolutionized how we handle files and collaborate. Throughout this book, we've delved into the vast array of Google Drive features, from crafting and exchanging files to real-time teamwork.

We've offered hands-on instances and easy-to-follow guidelines to help you truly grasp Google Drive, refining your work efficiency. Furthermore, we've delved into more advanced subjects like add-ons, streamlining tasks, and weaving Google apps together to propel your productivity to new heights.

With Google Drive, your files are accessible from any location and device, enabling seamless collaboration in real-time. Whether you're a student, a businessperson, or simply aiming to organize your files better, Google Drive equips you with the necessary tools.

We sincerely hope this book has proven to be a valuable companion, aiding you in fully utilizing the potential of Google Drive. Keep in mind that the possibilities with Drive are boundless—so keep exploring and unearthing innovative methods to collaborate and handle files. Thank you for embarking on this journey with us, and we extend our best wishes for all your future endeavors.

www.ingramcontent.com/pod-product-compliance
Lightning Source LLC
LaVergne TN
LVHW051716050326
832903LV00032B/4238